BEDFORDSHIRE

by

DENNIS BIDWELL

COUNTRYSIDE BOOKS

NEWBURY · BERKSHIRE

First published 2000
© Dennis Bidwell 2000

COUNTRYSIDE BOOKS
3 Catherine Road
Newbury, Berkshire

To view our complete range of books,
please visit us at
www.countrysidebooks.co.uk

ISBN 1 85306 640 0

Produced through MRM Associates Ltd., Reading
Typeset by Techniset Typesetters, Merseyside
Printed by Woolnough Bookbinding Ltd., Irthlingborough

CONTENTS

Now a bicycle shed, this useful outbuilding was the author's boyhood privy.

FOREWORD

Getting out of bed on a cold winter's night and putting your nice warm bum on a freezing lavatory seat down the garden is something you never forget. In my case this is just as well for, in collecting privy stories around the county, my own real-life experience was a definite advantage.

Our old privy, or lav as it was commonly called in Bedfordshire, must have encouraged constipation because we needed laxatives only in winter. Some privies were cosy but not ours. Widely spaced louvre windows, aimed at dispersing smells, also allowed driving rain or swirling snow to end up on the wooden seat.

Everything changed in the summer: suddenly the old privy was not so bad. As the door opened inwards you could sit and watch the day, knowing it could be kicked shut if you heard footsteps approaching. Often it was a place of sanctuary from a promised 'clip of the ear' following a misdemeanour, or sometimes just a place to be alone, away from the bustle of a big family. Contemplation in a privy is best described in the well known ditty:

> Sometimes I sits and thinks
> and sometimes I sits and stinks
> other times I just sits.

In the Mid Bedfordshire village of Maulden where I was raised there was no mains sewerage until the 1960s so, apart from a few cesspit owners, we all had a bucket privy, emptied by the council's contractors once a week. If more frequent emptying was needed, perhaps due to visitors, a hole in the garden served the same purpose. These primitive sanitary arrangements could sometimes come as a shock to city children,

5

never instructed in rural delights. A young evacuee in the village found the procedure so distasteful he would never miss an opportunity to lecture me on the virtues of the Royal Doulton WC, installed at his house 'in town'. He belaboured the point to such a degree I believed it must have been truly 'Royal' and decided when I grew up and left home I would tell anybody who asked that we had a Royal Doulton. I am still waiting for someone to ask!

To enable me to get even with this lad for showing off, an older boy wrote a poem for me to copy onto our privy wall:

> Down this hole deep and smelly
> Lies Terry the Twerp up to his belly
> Just leave him there put the bolt on
> He wont flush this like a Royal Doulton.

The joke misfired because Terry never saw it and I had to scrub it off, which I thought was a pity.

A favourite place to be at this time was my uncle's farm, under the guise of helping out. The little wooden privy there was clinker-built and always smelled of creosote. It perched on the edge of a stream where, some fifteen feet below, wild ducks swam in the shallow water.

Through gorging myself on Victoria plums I ended up in the privy early one morning just as the cows came wandering into the farmyard, mooing to be milked. One of them called Shirley, always curious, came round the back of the house and tried to squeeze past the privy. At the first creak I was off the seat and pulling up my shorts. I tried to open the door but her big body was in the way as it opened outwards. I had visions of ending up in the water with privy and bucket to boot, all because of one nosy cow. Fortunately by banging her flanks with the door and using some of my uncle's choice words, I persuaded her to saunter off and I was out of that privy in a flash.

So much for *my* privy tales, but would people tell me theirs? I confess to a few misgivings at first; after all, lavatorial experiences are not high on the list of topics in normal conversation. As it was, the people of Bedfordshire I met on my travels, and others who wrote or 'phoned, went out of their way to help by sharing their memories and spreading the word. Old photographs were dug out and a man from Flitwick even gave me an unused lavatory bucket as a memento. So, to all you generous-hearted people too numerous to acknowledge individually, I dedicate this book on Bedfordshire privies because without your help, and that of my wife and her PC, it could never have been written. Perhaps it should be read in the smallest room in the interests of contemplation.

DENNIS BIDWELL

[1]

PRIVIES OF THE PAST

Compared to our love affair with food, sanitation has always been a pain in the backside, an expense nobody wanted. For centuries it was left to the individual to get rid of his own waste and he, in turn, wanted it out of his house, even if this meant into open street drains. Servants found overhanging upstairs windows ideally suited for emptying slop pails and chamber pots – it being considered etiquette in some places to first shout a warning cry, 'gardy loo' from the French 'gardez l'eau' meaning watch the water. Not very helpful for the less than nimble or hard of hearing.

In an effort to cleanse our streets some councils in the 16th century started fining the worst offenders and also appointed scavengers to clean up the worst of the mess. Unfortunately they were not employed on a Sunday and that was the time when families used the streets most – attending church or visiting friends.

From a law dating back to 1189, cesspits were not allowed to be too close to a neighbour's property but in practice this rule was often ignored. The Assize of Nuisance dealt with cases where cesspits had been permitted, or even diverted, into the cellars of neighbour's houses. Other cases concerned piles of odorous muck stacked up and oozing through the next door's brickwork.

The men who cleaned out cesspits were either called 'gong-fermers', an old Saxon word, or 'rakers'. One known as 'Richard the Raker' must have been very neglectful of his own cesspit for he fell through the rotten planking in 1326 and drowned 'monstrously in his own excrement'. Some years before, another

'Gardy loo' – this Hogarth illustration of 1738 shows the hazards for passers-by when the chamber pots were being emptied!

unfortunate man, simply known as the 'Jew of Tewkesbury', also fell into a cesspit but because it was Saturday, his Sabbath, he would not allow anyone to pull him out, so great was his devotion. On hearing about this, the Earl of Gloucester, in respect of his own Sabbath which was on Sunday, would not allow him to be pulled out on that day either. Come Monday morning the poor devout man was dead.

A cesspit outside Newgate jail in London contained a massive 20 tons of accumulated filth. It took a gang of 12 men a week to clear it and they are said to have been paid quite generously but, what is equally certain, they were not overpaid.

The word 'midden' was given to accumulated excrement and similar waste, so perhaps the Middle Ages, should have been called the 'Midden Ages', because it was certainly an age of the 'muck hole'. At one time in Bedford there were reckoned to be 3,000 of these, many so close to wells they were polluting the drinking water.

One of the problems was that the gong-fermers, scavengers or anybody else had to dispose of human waste somewhere. With a growing population the volume of waste was increasing rapidly whilst disposal places were dwindling. Anybody near a river dumped their waste in there until that too became a sewer but, at the same time, many people relied on rivers to supply drinking water, so disease flourished.

Roman expertise had not rubbed off on us even though they were here for nearly four centuries. They adored cleanliness in all its forms and were so open about bodily functions they had no need for euphemisms. For instance in Tudor times a lady wishing to use the toilet would go to 'pluck a rose'. Going to the toilet in public would always have been abhorrent to the English who even invented the word 'privy', from the Latin 'privatus' meaning private or secret.

To the Romans going to the loo was a social occasion and an

A Roman latrine – note the open-fronted seats for inserting the sponge sticks which were then washed in the small channels of running water in the floor. More water flowed beneath the seats.

11

appropriate time to give thanks to Crepitas, god of the loo, or to Stercutius, god of excrement. The remains of a common latrine at Housesteads on the Roman Wall at Northumberland shows there were sufficient seats to accommodate up to 20 persons, all bent on relieving themselves at the same time. Seats were arranged along two walls so that everybody faced inwards in the interests of sociability. Down below water flushed away the waste through stone gullies and more water ran along narrow channels in the floor where small sponges on sticks, in place of toilet paper, could be rinsed clean after use ready for the next person. It paid not to get hold of 'the wrong end of the stick' in those days.

Traces of a similar communal latrine were found during excavation of the Roman city of Verulamium at St Albans just a few miles from the Bedfordshire border. Sanitary-wise it was a sad day when the Romans went home in AD 410. It seems it was left to the innovative Victorians to come up with a suitable tribute and this they did when they circulated versions of a prayer to the goddess of sewers, Cloacina, to hang in countless toilets throughout the land:

> Fair Cloacina, goddess of this place
> Where relief is given to the human race
> Graciously grant my offering may flow
> Not rudely swift, nor obstinately slow.

The Saxon hordes who arrived after the Romans were very different. Cleanliness was not their thing, in fact they despised it. Some religious leaders spoke out against washing, which was a luxury they devoutly denied themselves – even though Christianity was bound up with baptism and the cleansing effect of immersion. As for calls of nature, the one rule was it should only be done 'a bow shot from the nearest house'. If their King,

Elstow Abbey was built close to water, as was Chicksands Priory.

Edmund Ironsides, had done that, in 1016, instead of using a privy he might have escaped an assassin who watched him enter, waited until he was nicely settled, then thrust a spear into his rear end 'wherehaf kyng Edmunde died shortly after.'

Cleanliness was taken very seriously by the monks who as a result lived far healthier lives than the average person. This was due to their use of water from rivers or streams which by design invariably flowed alongside abbeys and monasteries. Their latrines, called reredorters, rere for rear and dorter meaning dormitory, were ideally sited over water so that waste could be washed away. There is a convenient water supply adjacent to the ruins of Elstow Abbey, and Chicksands Priory is equally well favoured.

Some monasteries had quite extensive reredorters, each seat

13

shielded from the next either out of modesty or decency or perhaps because quiet contemplation was preferred to open conversation in those cloistered enclaves. For his personal use, the Abbot of St Albans had rainwater from the roof diverted to a stone cistern and from there it flushed his toilet. It was a most ingenious idea considering this was early in the 12th century.

Privies in castles were called garderobes, a similar word to wardrobe and meaning almost the same thing, a small closet. Some were built jutting out from the walls of castles so that all the human waste ended up in the moat, if there was one. This arrangement must have been most uncomfortable for the users on a cold windy day and the splattering down the castle walls not a pretty sight. Another design was more elaborate and less conspicuous. Shafts, or chutes, ran from under the seat in the garderobe, down through the middle of the massive walls to a cesspit in the bowels of the castle – out of sight out of mind.

By their very nature garderobes were meant for single occupancy and not for a whole crowd such as the one that gathered in the garderobe of German Emperor, Frederick Barbarossa. They followed him once too often for the floor gave way under their weight and several plummeted to their deaths in the cesspit below. The Emperor managed to grab a rail and this saved his life. Not so fortunate was our own Edward II, whose wife, with her lover and fellow conspirators, cast him into the stinking garderobe pit at Berkeley Castle, Gloucestershire, in 1327. It was hoped he would die of some disease or other during the weeks he was kept there, but he survived so they murdered him.

A king who seems to have had a more sensitive nose than most was Henry III. He rebuilt garderobes and privies in many of his properties because he found the smell from the old ones unbearable. The stench of dirty water coming from his kitchens at Westminster Palace also bothered him because he thought it might be injurious to visitors' health. To cure the problem he had a system of drains built between the kitchen and the Thames which was very innovative at that time.

Advice for home owners of the Middle Ages was given by one Dr Andrew Boorde: 'Beware of draughty privies and pyssyng in draughts, and permyt no common pyssyng place about the house – and let the common place of easement be over some water or else elongated from the house. Beware of emptying pysse pottes, and pyssing in chymnes.'

Chymnes (chimneys) were fireplaces which could be massive in the larger houses in those days and a quick pee amongst the ashes must have been very convenient for busy servants – even if the smell of drying urine was offensive.

There would have been no excuse for 'pyssing in chymnes' at Hampton Court Palace for it contained Henry VIII's 'great house of easement' which sported 28 seats, a choice of two levels and the knowledge that, instead of a foul cesspit, the waste ended up in the Thames via a proper drainage system – regularly scrubbed clean by small boys. These loos were no longer called 'garderobes' or 'privies', now they were the 'jakes' but, whatever they were called, they were not used by the King. Like the monarchs who followed him, Henry VIII preferred his 'close stool' which was an ornately covered padded box containing a bucket and a small tank of water. It followed him everywhere, even on his travels. For the King it was a most comfortable arrangement – but not all that pleasant for the servant who attended him.

It might well be said that royal attachment to the 'close stool' and the 'stool room' where they were kept, delayed the development of the flush toilet. As early as 1596, Queen Elizabeth I's godson, Sir John Harington, designed and installed a WC at his home in Somerset which so impressed the Queen she had one put into Richmond Palace.

Nothing came of his invention and, although Queen Anne had a marble seat of 'easement' washed down with water at

The moat around picturesque Moretaine Manor is only a step away from the former privies around the back.

Windsor Castle, it was not until 1775 that the idea of a WC was taken up again. This time by Alexander Cummings, a London clock-maker, who obtained a patent for his invention which included the ingenious S-bend for keeping sewer smell at bay which we use today.

Generally this WC was efficient but there was an occasional valve problem. This was corrected within three years by Joseph Bramah whose product then set the standard for the next century. The quality of his workmanship was so high he received the distinction of having his name become part of everyday language in describing something that was the best – a real 'bramah'.

With the invention of the WC it might have seemed that the following poem from 1697 called *Piss-Potts Farewell* was at last applicable:

> Presumptuous pisse-pot, how did'st thou offend?
> Compelling females on their hams to bend?
> To kings and queens we humbly bend the knee
> But queens themselves are forced to stoop to thee.

Yet the chamber pot still had a long way to go before it became obsolete. Mains water was making flush toilets possible – in better off houses – but sewers were few and far between. Where they did not exist cesspools overflowed into ditches, gullies and gardens, and an ever increasing town population made things as bad as ever. In the cities 'night soil men', with a barrel suspended on a pole between them, cleared cesspits under lamplight when flies were less of a nuisance and the smell less noticeable.

Small towns suffered too and, as late as 1872, the medical officer for Ampthill, Dr Henry Holland, once surgeon to the Duke of Wellington, was pressing for action in his reports. One criticism concerned the common practice of using storm channels as

Once every bedroom had a chamber pot, usually under the bed, hence the nickname 'gozunder'.

sewers which led to his conclusion about the water closet, 'that it had nothing to recommend it as every condition considered essential to health is violated.'

1842 was an important date in loo history: a WC was installed at Buckingham Palace and Edwin Chadwick's report on the 'Sanitary Conditions of the Labouring Population of Great Britain' was published. It showed quite clearly the correlation between poor health and bad sanitation. In Toddington for instance it was revealed that people suffering from fever were living in cottages where few had usable privies and there was a stinking dung heap outside nearly every door where 'every species of filth was accumulated.'

In towns it was not unusual to find the poor had no sanitary arrangements at all or that dozens of people were sharing a

18

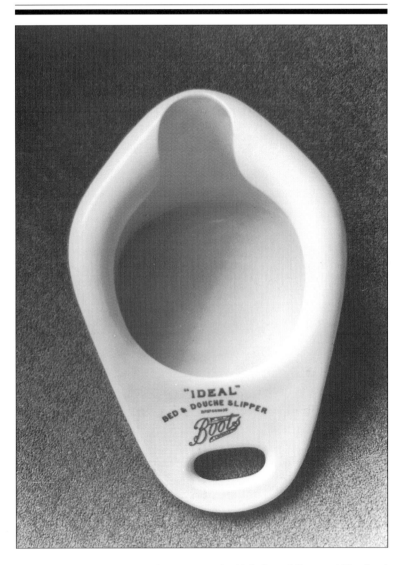

If you could not get up, a bedpan was used which, hopefully, would be fitted with a flannel sleeve for additional comfort.

Chamber pot manufacturers were not without a sense of humour.

single privy often over an un-maintained cesspit. Disease was rampant as sources of drinking water became contaminated. Our towns and cities reeked and the child mortality rate soared.

At last in 1848 we had the first Public Health Act that, amongst other things, made it compulsory for every *new* house to have either a flush loo, a privy or a pit. Sanitary reform was in the air but progress was painfully slow. A decade passed and then Parliament itself was brought to a standstill by the unbearable stench of the Thames. A year later and a huge sewerage scheme was under way in London.

Throughout the land progress depended upon the authorities' willingness to spend money, which meant higher rates for householders, including themselves. In Oliver Street, Ampthill, for instance, the residents petitioned the Rural Sanitary Authority

The 18th century Bowling Green House and Pavilion at Wrest Park contain two-holers with large vaults beneath.

Substantial outbuildings near Old Warden provided wash-houses and privies for two dwellings.

in 1879 for a sewer, or at least a drain, but the Ampthill committee decided it was unnecessary. At the same time they complained about soap suds getting into the street.

Eventually all towns and cities got their WCs and sewers but as late as 1900 there was still ten per cent of Londoners without mains water to the house, let alone an inside loo. In Bedford-shire, as with the other shire counties, houses were still being built with outside privies, right up to World War Two, which is why there are so many people who can remember the trip down the garden path to the outside lav – just what this book is all about.

[2]

FROM NOSEGAYS TO
ROYAL DOULTONS

In bygone days ladies would have reached for their nosegays believing the best way to cover a stink was with a smell. It was common practice to let sweet smelling plants like honeysuckle climb up privies for the same reason. Not that every lady used a privy, many preferred their commode or even a bed pan which so angered Jonathan Swift (1667-1745) he wrote his scathing *Directions to Servants* to shame them:

'I am very much offended with those ladies, who are so proud and lazy, that they will not be at the pains of stepping into the garden to pluck a rose, but keep an odious implement, sometimes in the bedchamber itself, or at least in a dark closet adjoining, which they make use of to ease their worst necessities; and you are the usual carriers away of the pan, which maketh not only the chamber, but even their clothes offensive, to all who come near. Now, to cure them of the odious practice, let me advise you, on whom this office lieth, to convey away this utensil, that you will do it openly, down the great stairs, and in the presence of the footmen: and if anybody knocketh, to open the street door, while you have the vessel in your hands: this, if anything can, will make your lady take the pains of evacuating her person in the proper place, rather than expose her filthiness to all the men servants in the house.'

Relieving themselves has always been easier for men than women, who suffered terrible discomfort before public toilets were introduced. When the Great Exhibition building was erected in Hyde Park in 1851 by 'Bedfordshire boy made good' Joseph Paxton, it was decided to install WCs in the rest rooms.

Lucky find at Ampthill – a commode that doubles-up as a step stool, demonstrated here by Sue Melville.

Incredibly, objections were raised but George Jennings, the designer, was allowed to go ahead anyway. Not all ladies dared use the new fangled contraptions but thousands did and it proved such a commercial success it followed the Crystal Palace to Sydenham.

Thanks to George Jennings the public loo had arrived and he went on to install them in many of our towns and cities – aptly described as 'Temples of Convenience' by Lucinda Lampton in her excellent book. We were beginning to catch up with the Romans who had public toilets in their cities centuries before and they were free – until Emperor Vespasian, who ordered the building of the Colosseum, not only made the public pay but then sold the urine to the wool trade.

Urine has always had its uses: in the north of England in the 19th century it was collected in a drum and shared amongst the contributors on washday for putting in with the clothes. It is also legendary for curing chilblains and in Bedford Record Office there is a lovely description of two maids, sitting on their beds, taking turns to soak their feet after using the chamber pot.

Mrs Winter from Bedford tells me she never suffered from chilblains but frequently had a foot in the chamber pot as a child because her sister would forget to put it back under the bed. Stains on the ceiling below told their own tale in the cottage. One night when she was very small, she crept into her parents' bed after waking up frightened. Unfortunately she promptly wet their bed and, when it finally dawned on her father that he had got the brunt of it, he jumped bolt upright and shouted 'She's wet the bed.' His sudden movement caused the leg of the bedstead to go straight through the floorboards and they all ended up in a heap on the floor.

In our public loos circular urinals appeared which were very efficient space savers and another ingenious idea from George Jennings. Thomas Twyford produced a lavatory pan free from

Not a 'Crapper' but a well-respected Twyford 'Deluge', this one has been in daily use since 1899.

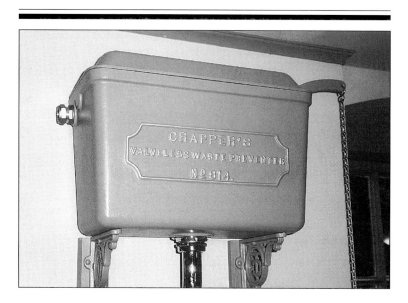

Crapper solved the problem! (Photo courtesy of Simon Kirby)

its wooden constraints which came as quite a shock. It had always been discreetly boxed in and now it was suddenly revealed as a pedestal of refinement, clean and shiny, shapely and decorative. It took some getting used to but the medical profession helped by promoting its hygienic qualities.

But lavatory pans are only as good as the cistern that governs them. What was badly needed in the 19th century was a good flush of water to do the job, which switched off afterwards and could not be left running. Thomas Crapper solved the problem with his 'Valveless Water Waste Preventer' which was so good we still use it today. His biography is by Wallace Reyburn and entitled *Flushed with Pride*. Thomas can be credited with giving us the cistern but not the WC nor the word 'crap', that was around long before he was born in 1837.

'By Special Appointment' – some Royal Doultons.

In spite of his marvellous invention, with world-wide application, he was never very famous in this country but the Americans gave him a posthumous accolade by taking his cistern back to their country after the First World War. They had nothing like it and the 'crapper' cistern spread across the States until 'going to the crapper' became a recognised euphemism almost like our 'spending a penny'.

The word 'crap' returned to these shores, meaning nonsense or rubbish and seems to have resurrected our own ancient word which could mean defecate, hence we get the schoolboy phrase for sounding your 'r's.

> The Cat Crept into the Crypt
> Crapped and Crept out again.

This circulated after the Second World War which makes the meaning of the word quite clear, even though not acceptable in polite society – old English or not.

An Ampthill lady told me that many years ago she lived next door to an American serviceman's wife, the mother of two beautiful little girls. The children used to come into her garden to play and she loved having them. It bothered her that they used the word 'crap' when they needed the toilet so she spoke diplomatically to their mother who agreed it was not a nice word for children to use and she would talk to them. From then on they said 'poop' instead which the lady in question thought even worse so she made no further suggestions.

[3]

PEOPLE'S PRIVIES

At 96 years old Chris Creamer of Milton Bryan has done his fair share of carrying buckets because he still had a privy in the 1980s. Years before the council took on the job of bucket emptying Chris would plan his garden so that he knew where the next bucketful was going. In this way, over a period of time, the whole garden benefited and, in turn, so did Chris's family through the good quality vegetables it produced.

Chris worked as a farmhand all his life, which was a healthy occupation compared to factories in those days but the hours were even longer: from 6 am to 6 pm on Monday to Friday and 4 pm on Saturday in all weathers. 'There was a privy for the workers at the farmyard but there was no going back once you were in the fields. Then it was a five minutes squat behind a hedge, if you could find one, and finishing the job off with a handful of grass or leaves in place of the usual paperwork.'

Chris's workmate from Woburn, a single fellow who kept himself to himself, had quite a fright when he went to his privy one night. He opened the door and there in the lamplight sat this woman just looking at him. Poor chap didn't know what to do so he slammed the door and ran back into his cottage, still bursting to use his privy. He dare not speak to her in case she started shouting and caused a disturbance. What would the neighbours think he was doing with a woman in his privy? He visualised all sorts of embarrassment – in the end, now quite desperate to relieve himself, he rushed upstairs, opened the small bedroom window that overlooked the privy and shouted at the top of his voice, 'I'm coming down there to use my privy whether there is anybody in there or not.' A few moments passed then he saw a

A typical privy bucket – note the deep body and small handle designed to prevent splashing.

shadowy figure slink away and he ran down to his privy – thankfully.

Chris never minded the old privy days but he's glad he is on the main sewer now otherwise, as he got older, he might have found the bucket too much to carry. 'The biggest trouble with privies was the gaps they put over and under the door to give plenty of ventilation. It was alright in the summer but swirling snow in the winter used to get in and settle on the seat.'

At nearby Eversholt, Shirley Gulliver remembered when her son David was about three years old. 'He was a bright inquisitive child who was never happier than when he was helping grown-ups. On the particular day in question they had visited his

A barn and a privy for each house under a common roof in Milton Bryan. Note the gap over the privy door.

grandma to take her shopping with them. Grandma never took the back door key with her because it was a big clumsy thing so she used to leave it on the seat of the privy under an upturned flower-pot. Young David knew where she kept it and, when they got back from shopping, he left the ladies at the gate and ran as fast as he could to the privy to get Grandma's key. Unfortunately it slipped straight through his fingers and into the nearly full bucket where it disappeared. Poor Grandma had to retrieve it to get into the house and she couldn't face having her tea that night.'

Another Eversholt lady remembered calling the council tanker the 'violet' cart and believed people were still using buckets as

A neatly built privy at Roxon House, Toddington, hardly noticeable at the far end of a large garden.

late as 1985 in some places. Before this everybody emptied their own and it was the caretaker's job to empty the school buckets, all six of them. The only place he could find to dig so many holes so frequently was the allotments which were a fair distance away. To ease his burden he used a milkman's yoke across his shoulders and clipped two buckets on at a time, letting the chain take the strain. Even so it was not a good idea to walk behind him.

At Houghton Conquest there used to be a row of cottages with only one small privy down the garden shared between four families. The lady who was telling me this story was one of five children and her family was the smallest. 'With so many people using it, not only did the bucket need to be emptied all the time, but there always seemed to be somebody in there when you were bursting to go yourself which was quite often because it was a long walk down there on a cold night and you tended to put it off until the last minute.'

One night when she was only ten years old she made her way down to the privy in moonlight, crept inside and settled herself down on the seat. As she did so, something scurried across the seat behind her, dropped on the floor and went out under the door. She screamed and all the cottage doors opened as the neighbours peered out. Her grandfather came to her aid and confirmed her worst fear that it was a rat she had nearly put her bare behind on.

From then on she would never go down there without a good light but, quite often, just as she got seated, she would hear scratching on the wooden door and was terrified the old rat was trying to get in. Eventually her mischievous brother got his ears boxed for doing it purposely to frighten her – brothers were like that.

A Luton resident, Mrs Townrow, also remembers living in a tiny cottage in a row of four and having to share the privy. Admittedly it was a two-holer so sometimes the girls kept each other company. This was a blessing because the holes were both adult size and, instead of a bucket underneath, it was just a pit. She was always afraid she would fall through and not be able to get out. One day she was in the middle of 'doing her business' and suddenly there was a rush of cold air coming from underneath. 'I could hear the sound of shovelling and did not know whether to finish off, or leave my backside where it was and hope the man had not noticed.' It was an embarrassment she has remembered for over 60 years.

Mrs Burrows now lives at Flitwick but was originally at Mill Lane, Greenfield, where her father bought two cottages and made them into one house. 'This meant we had two privies and both were two-holers, a large one for adults and a small one for children so we were well catered for in that respect, but they were quite different – one had a bucket to be emptied on the garden, the other was a pit privy built to slope into the neighbour's garden strangely enough. This was an arrangement between the previous owner and our neighbour who hoped it would carry on. My father was more than happy about this and periodically our neighbour would set to work with a shovel and move the accumulated contents of this privy onto his garden. We hardly ever used the other one because we did not want to deprive him.'

A bonus in searching for old privies lies in discovering interesting houses like Philip Strickland's historical home at Riseley. Early sanitary arrangements for this 15th century residence remain a mystery but a pit was found outside containing various layers of ash and other materials which might have been a pit privy. Further round the house is a door on the first floor with no access to it from the outside, which is another puzzle. Could it have been the inside door of a garderobe? Alas, it seems we can only speculate.

In North Bedfordshire, Brian Phillips of Melchbourne told me his house used to be two cottages and showed me the former joint privy building. Around the back, under a neat brick archway, were two concrete squares in the floor with a metal ring in the middle for heaving them upwards. They were pit privies and periodically had to be shovelled out and the contents put into the garden.

This was quite a problem because the cottages were set so far

The mystery door on Philip Strickland's house. Part of a garderobe perhaps?

A privy at Moretaine Manor – note the vertical slots in the door, an unusual method of ventilation.

back from the road they had no back garden to speak of and in the large front garden was their well, the only source of drinking water – which two privy loads of 'manure' could easily contaminate. It was always a headache and it was a great day when the council sealed up the holes under the privy seats and installed buckets which were emptied weekly by the contractors.

As a small boy Brian lived at another cottage which had a two-hole privy. His uncle was living with them and the two men would wander down to the privy in the evening to attend to their personal business and at the same time enjoy a good smoke and a manly chat. If it seemed they had been gone longer than usual Brian would be sent down the garden to undo the trapdoor at the back of the privy and pretend he had a handful of thistles. It never failed to get them out of there.

Eventually Brian joined the army and was stationed in Nottinghamshire, miles from anywhere. Here they used large containers which the troops nicknamed 'thunder-buckets' and there was just one for each hut so they had to be emptied every day. Fortunately at this camp the army employed a contractor to do the job and he would turn up the same time every morning in a gorgeous Austin 1800 car, the sort that men could envy knowing that few people could afford one in those days. Behind his new car he towed a trailer full of large barrels and he would drive up and down the rows of huts emptying each bucket in turn then slowly drive away. Brian reckoned this was the best example he has ever seen to illustrate the truism 'where there's muck there's money'.

[4]

JUST THE JOB

Privies, like houses, come in all shapes and sizes. One of the grandest is probably the 'Temple' at the back of Hinwick House, the magnificent Queen Anne mansion in the parish of Podington. Here was a four-seater – it is currently being restored – that had a decorative alcove built across each corner, giving the interior of the building a hexagonal shape. Each of the four occupants would have sat back in their own ornate niche on a wooden seat facing the centre, in full view of the others. It must have seemed to the users like a public loo from Roman times, except there was no water, just a deep pit underneath for the droppings.

There were different types of pit privy. Some small ones just accumulated waste until they were full up then another pit was dug, and the family moved their privy to a new site and started all over again. Permanent pit privies had to be shovelled out periodically or, more appropriately, the contents ladled out with a long-handled scoop specially made for the job. Some Luton workmen in 1945 were observed to be using a scoop of their own design, a frying pan lashed to a broom handle. This was when the River Lea had got so contaminated one resident described it as 'more like a sewer than a river'.

A more elaborate, and efficient, pit privy was of the 'dry' type, sometimes called a 'vault'. It usually had a sloping concrete base and bricked up walls that finished at an archway. Liquid drained out but a mound of earth against the archway kept the main waste inside and dry. When shovelled out it was well mixed with earth and fairly innocuous. In order to keep as much liquid out of the vault as possible, when males did not need to sit down, they were expected to find a suitable spot outside.

After restoration, the four-seater 'Temple' at Hinwick House, Hinwick, will be a magnificent example of 18th century craftsmanship.

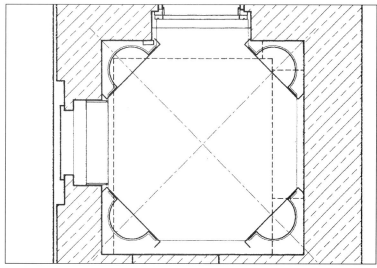

'In full view of the others' – plan courtesy of Meridian Design.

MOULE'S EARTH CLOSETS

Apparatus on Bearers ready to Fix.
Deal Seat 3' 0" Long.

No. A1724. " Pull Out," as drawn.
No. A1725. " Pull Up " Pattern.
No. A1726. " Self-acting " Pattern.

Strong, Portable, Self-Contained Set. Plain Deal. Galvanized Fittings. Pail complete. 21" Wide. 27" Back to Front.

No. A1727. " Pull Out."
(as drawn)

No. A1728. " Pull Up "

Strong, Portable, Self-contained.
Best Plain Deal.
Fittings of Galvanized Iron.
With Pail complete.

No. A1729. Self-Acting. 21" Wide.
27" Back to Front. 36" High.

No.		
A1724	..	.. 57/6
A1725	..	.. 70/-
A1726	..	.. 100/-
*A1727	..	.. 72/6
*A1728	..	.. 86/6
*A1729	..	.. 102/6

* Pails included.
Other Pails **3/7** Each Extra.

The Reverend Moule's earth closets of 1860 were still being produced in the 1930s and thousands were sold at home and abroad.

When the ingenious Reverend Henry Moule from Dorset discovered by experiment how quickly animal and human waste broke down in dry earth he filled in his own offensive cesspit and switched to a bucket. Then, in 1860, he brought out the Moule Patented Earth Closet. In its simplest form this was just a bucket under a wooden frame with a hopper at the back which contained dry earth. It was operated by the pull of a lever which allowed a pound or two of dry earth to drop into the bucket to cover up the contents.

It was very successful and thousands of Moules were sold world-wide. They provided an acceptable solution whilst people waited for the coming of sewers and WCs. Not that the Reverend Moule accepted the WC was superior to his creation, and he spent years arguing in its favour. The trouble with it, however, was twofold: firstly only dry earth could be used if it was to work properly – for which they even sold earth-drying heaters – and, secondly, an ordinary family of six people would use two tons of earth each year. This all had to be man-handled into the hopper and out into the bucket, which was a far cry from the convenience of a flush toilet in spite of the Reverend's conviction.

Various improvements to the Moule appeared including an automatic version which operated as the user rose from the sitting position. A spring under the seat activated the hopper mechanism, making it a hands-free operation. Not every person was interested in buying a Moule and the 'bucket and chuckit' method was still the most common, especially when it was emptied by somebody like Mr Ivan Walker who used to work on the Ampthill Rural District Council's tanker lorries that went round the villages emptying privy buckets.

Ivan told me that there were two men to each tanker and the one he drove in the 1950s was an old Bedford which had no heater in the cab or demister on the windscreen, so they improvised with candles stuck to the dashboard with tallow. In winter,

Elegant Shuttleworth mansion where even the loos are encased in mahogany.

by the time they got to the outlying villages like Ridgemont or Eversholt they felt half frozen and it was sheer luxury to linger briefly in the houses where they had to carry the buckets through the kitchen and the front room.

The normal routine was for operators to take their own bucket to the privy and transfer the contents of the householder's bucket to their own. Where houses were in rows, often with a common yard, two at a time could be managed. It could be hazardous, though, what with the combined weight of two full buckets and narrow or slippery paths, there was always that dread of slipping over followed by the big clean-up job. Overfull buckets were always a menace, because they so easily splashed about when being carried. One moment's carelessness could mean a squelching wellington-boot, and a lot of discomfort.

Ivan remembered emptying one bucket from a privy which had a trapdoor at the rear, not knowing there was a lady inside. All he heard was a squeal as a rush of cold air announced his presence but whatever she thought about the intrusion into her most private function nothing was ever mentioned.

The buckets were carried to the back of the tanker, where there was a hopper, and poured in. Ivan explained the working of the system: 'Ideally the contents would be got rid of in one go but a heavy frost could make it more difficult. The hopper had a lever at the side which controlled the suction and it slowed the job down if it kept getting jammed up. Then it would need blowing back very carefully, for the operator's sake. One particular tanker had the lever away from the hopper and the chap operating that had to be trusted completely.' Ivan remembered suffering a drenching from one heavy handed mate so he got his own back, he thought, but it was no victory because they had to travel home together in the cab.

Ivan accepted being gently ostracised when he was in his working clothes, as part of the job. Some people would jokingly

Mr Ivan Walker, who is now retired, pictured here with the tanker lorry he used to drive.

hold their nose when they saw him, or sometimes pull a face, but they were always pleased to see him round their house. He had heard the various expressions for his tanker, such as the 'lavender' or 'violet' wagon, but many people he knew just called it the 'poop' cart.

Helping his mum one day got Ivan and his mate the sack. Having heard that her drain was blocked, in a village a few miles away, Ivan went to her aid in his tanker, which was well equipped to sort the problem out. Unfortunately a mishap on the way back put the tanker in a ditch and the council were alerted. As the contents had to be drained into the ditch to lighten the load, road recovery was not a pleasant operation. Fortunately the dismissal proved to be a temporary affair and the pair were soon reinstated.

Ivan said, 'Driving these old tankers was not that easy, they were very basic. They held about 1,000 gallons and if you just touched the brakes there would be this terrific bang from inside as the contents smashed into the foremost bulk-head. Sometimes the force was so great it seemed the tanker would burst and cover the whole vehicle in sewage.'

Emptying cesspools was another part of the job. Suction pipes would be unreeled and inserted through a manhole cover. One day Ivan's mate was not looking where he was going, tripped over the pipe and went straight in – fortunately only up to his neck. Getting him out was a very messy business and he just had to be hosed down where he stood. As soon as that job was finished he had to be taken home for a change of clothes and the cab reeked.

Generally speaking, Ivan enjoyed his job on the tankers. He was able to work out of doors, meet a lot of nice people and have a day-shift job, unlike many men doing similar work at night. One thing Ivan is convinced about – there is no healthier occupation. He cannot remember ever catching so much as a cold.

Left alone for several years, this old privy in Maulden is typical of many in
its day.

[5]

COUNTRY SEAT TALES

Mr Reg West and his wife Gladys have lived at Gravenhurst since 1943, and at first they had a privy at the bottom of the garden which had a pit underneath instead of a bucket. When the pit needed cleaning out the first thing was to dig trenches in the garden then make sure all the windows in the house were tightly shut before the concrete slab was slid off the pit and the shovelling out started.

Some years later the council filled in the old pit privy and they had a bucket instead, which the council men emptied weekly. They turned up in what Gladys, and a lot of people, called the 'violet' wagon. Reg said that their cottage was from the 17th century and since that time there must have been an awful lot of manure put on the garden, which suddenly came to an end.'

Before they got married Reg lived with his parents at Pegsdon and they had a 'bucket and chuckit' system there. Unfortunately the garden was too small to find a fresh place to dig the hole every week so Reg's dad used to carry the bucket through the village at night to his allotment and bury it there. Reg's dad, like many other people with tiny gardens, blessed the day the council's bucket emptying scheme started.

Once when Gladys was staying the weekend, soon after they started courting, she needed to visit the privy at night. She quietly crept out of the kitchen door, anxious not to wake her future in-laws up, and found the privy in the dark. She felt that the door was ajar so she slipped inside and, just as she went to sit down, there was an almighty din with birds fluttering and squawking all over the place. Somebody had left the door open and the bantams had got in there to roost. Gladys not only woke her in-laws up, but people living nearby as well.

When Reg worked locally he often drove a tractor and trailer and one day was sent to Barton and told to move a farm labourer's things out of a cottage and into another one nearer Pegsdon. Reg explained: 'By the time I got there I needed the lav and the man said I could use theirs across the yard. It was mid-way between two cottages and when I got inside I found it was a two-holer. I told him how lucky he was because we only had a single-holer at home and I wondered if he and his wife went together? "That's not my two-holer," he told me, "the other one is our neighbour's. They are all the same along here. They are not two-holers for one family they are one-holers for two families – if you see what I mean." '

Over to Henlow where Mrs Ethel Cooper has a story to tell about her privy which was halfway down the garden.

'It has been converted to a coal shed now and the seat and bucket disposed of, but we used it for many years with the council contractors emptying it once a week. Sometimes it got filled up quicker than usual and then one of the men in the family had to deal with it.

'On one occasion, our daughter's young man, who was staying here at the time, volunteered to do the job, though he had never done it before. Unfortunately it was a bitter winter's day with sub-zero temperatures and it took him ages to dig any sort of hole, but he managed it at last and lugged the bucket out of the privy and over to the hole. He tipped it up but nothing came out because the top was frozen over. Before anybody could knock on the window to stop him, he put the bucket down then smashed through the ice with the spade. The contents shot out like a fountain all over his clothes and into his wellingtons. The poor lad was a real mess and the smell was dreadful – the hardest thing was keeping a straight face!'

50

A well designed pair of privies at Henlow.

Ethel and her late husband used to take local preachers home from the Methodist Chapel for tea if they were taking the evening service as well. To save them stumbling down the garden path in the dark she always put a lighted candle in a jam-jar in the privy. That outline of light from around the door has provided a guiding light for so many Methodist preachers over the years who graced Ethel's privy.

A story one of the preachers used to tell concerned a bald-headed Methodist preacher who was invited home for tea by an equally bald man in the congregation. When they got to the cottage where the man lived they were met by his wife who was not a church-goer herself and had very little to say.

The preacher badly needed to use the privy and when he looked through the kitchen window and saw the man of the house washing his hands at an outside tap he slipped out and asked him where the privy was. He was directed to the bottom of the garden and when he got back he also started washing his hands at the outside tap.

Suddenly he heard the kitchen window open and was shocked when a wet dishcloth hit him round the head. 'That's for bringing that old preacher home,' the lady snapped – clearly mistaking his bald head for her husband's.

When Olive Broad of Bedford was a little girl on her grand-father's farm she could never fathom why the privy was in the chicken-run. It meant you had to be careful not to leave the gate open and it got wet and muddy in the rain.

One day, acting on a whim, an aunt introduced tapioca pud-ding to the family which she insisted be eaten up. Unfortunately Olive never could stand it and, at the first chance, would always slip out the back door and give it to the chickens.

Soon, whenever she went to use the privy they would all come rushing over with wings flapping wanting food and the same

Still being used – Jim Bygraves from Northill has put his old privy bucket to good use.

thing happened when she came out of the privy. Nobody could understand this sudden interest in her and she couldn't own up.

Like many things years ago, galvanised lavatory buckets were built to last but eventually they needed replacing. For many people the first sign was when the bottom started to leak but others examined their buckets more often. Mrs Barbara Neale of Husborne Crawley knew a lady who always lined the bottom of her bucket with a few sheets of paper damped down with paraffin oil and others who put in a layer of cabbage leaves so that it emptied cleanly. Mrs Neale also remembered what happened to lavatory buckets whose bottom had rotted away – they went over the top of the rhubarb and brought it on a treat. Waste not want not.

Mr Jim Bygraves from Northill remembered the time a jackdaw used to poke his head through a hole in the privy roof, before it was re-tiled. The beautiful bird became a regular visitor and nobody took any notice of him peering down at them – perhaps comparing his method to ours.

One day, Jim's son, David, brought his wife home for the first time and it was obvious she had some trepidation about going down the garden. The first time she went she had just got settled on the seat when the jackdaw squawked and she looked up to see his beady eye on her. It was only when the family heard the commotion that they realised they had forgotten to tell her about their intruder.

When she was a little girl, Lynn Froggatt hated using the privy because she was always scared of falling into the pit underneath. On top of that a certain type of fly used to buzz about underneath so you always got a move on. The pit used to be emptied occasionally and then it was a question of all windows in the house being tightly shut. Later the awful pit was filled in and replaced by a bucket, which was a great improvement.

Unfortunately when the war came and took the men away it was left to her twelve year old brother Jim to deal with the bucket when it needed emptying. Digging the hole was alright but getting the bucket off the ground, even with two hands, was as much as he could manage and there were some mishaps. Jim went on to marry a London girl and, for her sake, he made his own privy immaculate, even to painting the seat white, but she remained aghast at using a lav that did not flush.

Handsome William Holden, the heart throb of so many cinemagoers, might have been pleased to know that a lady in Greenfield was so captivated by him after seeing *Sunset Boulevard* she painted the inside of her privy bright yellow and the door orange both sides, so she would always be reminded of him, and the film, whenever she sat on her throne.

Two charming ladies I met in Flitwick, Mrs Bunker and Mrs Robinson, told me they both lived in Toddington at one time, long before the main sewers arrived. Mrs Bunker recalled living at Earls Court Cottages, a grand name for a group of dwellings sharing a three-hole privy at the bottom of the garden. There were over thirty people regularly using the privy, not counting visitors, and it was frustrating to get all the way down there, especially in the rain, and have to wait your turn.

Every week a night soil man would come round and empty the buckets, and not a moment too soon. Children were in bed when he called so they used to watch from the bedroom window as he went up and down the garden path with a lantern in one hand and bucket in the other. He would disappear from view as he went to his tanker which was still horse-drawn at that time.

It was Mrs Robinson's father who had to empty their bucket

A Toddington scene: former Earls Court Cottages where privy space was at a premium.

early in the morning and, because he had a weak stomach, as far as that job was concerned, he put it off as long as possible. When he finally had to do it, he would fill up his old briar pipe to the limit and get it drawing really well, then, having already dug the hole, he would take a deep breath and be in and out of that privy in a flash, then off to work. He made sure nothing was ever grown in that part of the garden and any self sets, however bountiful, were left for the birds to enjoy.

When Mrs Robinson was a teenager she worked 'below stairs' at a large mansion in Ampthill and was constantly being startled by a life size cut-out figure that used to stand on the half landing. She kept forgetting it was there, then the gas lights would flicker and it would seem to come alive. These 'models' were used in large dining rooms, propped up against a chair, as the fourteenth guest in case only thirteen turned up which was an unlucky number, she understood.

One day she was sent upstairs to get a room ready for a visitor and found a square type of cupboard near the bed. Being young and curious, she opened it up and found it was a commode with the usual container inside but inside that was a china-clay model of a man's head. Was it some sort of joke? She often wondered but could never ask.

A story gleaned from a market trader in Bedford concerned a privy they used many years ago when his grown-up son was only four years old. One year early in October, the family got together and made a really professional guy for the forthcoming Guy Fawkes night celebrations.

To keep it dry they shoved it in the privy, which was a two-holer, a large hole for adults and a small one for children. Who-ever was using one seat would put 'Guy' on the other one so he was moved backwards and forwards with a few choice com-ments and some amusement, until the big night when they put him on top of the bonfire and set light to it.

All the children were enthralled except the little lad; he was distraught and frantically crying for somebody to get 'Guy' off the fire before he got burned and put him back in the privy. He was eventually placated but they never put another 'Guy' in the privy . . . and the little lad? He grew up to be a nice guy himself.

Mrs J. Stirling remembers, as an 18 year old 'townie', being taken to a farm at Eaton Bray by her fiancé to meet his family. Later, when she needed to go to the loo she was given his mother's wellingtons, plus a large torch, and pointed in the direction of a privy in the middle of an orchard.

She stumbled over to it and inside found the usual bench arrangement, with a hole in the seat, and next to it a sheet of

Newbury Manor, Silsoe, has an elaborate two-hole privy of the vault type, built on the edge of a moat. The users of this privy had the benefit of spaciousness and attractive panelled walls.

An excellent conversion, seen at Southill's old station, of two former privies, one each end of an outbuilding, that were once used by railwaymen and their families.

newspaper. So that she could use two hands she placed the torch on the newspaper and it promptly disappeared below because the privy was a two-holer!

'When I got back to the house and told my fiancé he came out with a pair of tongs, opened up the back and probed for the torch which was still shining. Seeing what was happening the dog jumped in as well only to be pulled out none to gently. This prompted it to run back into the house, through the open kitchen door, and do what all wet dogs do, shake itself everywhere.

'It was a struggle not to laugh at the comic situation but the stern faces helped.'

[6]

BOG STANDARDS

Modern times not only brought the lav into the house but also the dog. In the days of the privy down the garden, man's best friend stayed outside in a kennel at the end of a long length of chain. Unfortunately this meant it was often impossible to have a clear run to the privy. It was certainly no joke rushing down the garden on a wet and windy night, with a candle flickering in a jamjar, only to get tangled up in a dog's chain but it happened because of the geography of the average back yard.

A Houghton Conquest lady remembers as a child, having to steer a course between her family's labrador and the neighbour's collie. Their respective chains kept the creatures only two feet apart so at night she used to aim for a concrete bump in the middle of the back yard where an old well had been covered over. She became so skilful she could get through the gap without so much as a touch from a friendly wet nose but it was always a close thing. For men coming home from the pub it was a different matter.

Jack Bean from Luton also wrote about the dog problem: he used to visit a nice old pub in Woburn years ago where the 'gents' was outside down a yard. The trouble was an alsatian that was tied-up down there would not always let you pass, however badly you needed to. Other times he would stop you coming back just for devilment, or boredom, and you tended not to argue with him but wait for him to be distracted.

The cleaning of privies was a regular chore for wives or daughters and the bare wooden seats became almost white with continuous scrubbing. Spiders were both a blessing and a nuisance. They certainly kept down the flies, attracted to the

Mrs Margaret Anderson of Elstow outside her old privy with its new door.
Inside is the original seat and lid, also the old bucket.

bucket, but they sometimes ventured from their lair as a reminder that when you sat down they were underneath. It was best to move the bucket to get at the cobwebs and, when Mrs Trembling of Maulden was considered old enough to take on privy-cleaning for the first time this is what she did but then left it in full view of passers-by and had to have more instructions.

Strong disinfectant, on top of everything else, gave privies a special kind of smell. Certain shrubs planted outside also helped disguise the privy odour but it could have side effects as Jean Page of Clapham knows. Her mother, living at Queens Park, Bedford, cannot stand honeysuckle, which could be classed as a real family favourite in the top-ten of fragrances. This is because the privy she used as a child was covered in honeysuckle and now just one whiff brings back memories of that old privy smell.

Another reason shrubs were planted around privies was in the interest of modesty. Everybody used the privy but nobody wanted to be seen using it so a natural screen was welcomed, especially by the ladies. This was noted as far back as 1751 by Samuel Rolleston in his *Philosophical Dialogue Concerning Decency*: 'Our Ladies in England are ashamed of being seen even in going to or returning from the most necessary parts of our houses, as if it was itself shameful to do even in private what nature absolutely requires at certain seasons to be done; whereas I have known an old woman in Holland set herself on the next hole to a Gentleman and civilly offer him her mussel shell by way of a scraper after she had done with it herself.'

It was the availability of paper on a large scale that revolutionised our personal habits. Up until then it was 'any material at hand'. From nature's own, grass and leaves, to old habits which monks tore up for use in their reredorters. Newspaper became our national lavatory paper and people got attached to their favourites in more ways than one. Glossy magazines with plenty of pictures were more interesting, for the privy users, but often too thick and smooth to be effective. At least the ink stayed on the paper which was not always the case with some publications. Hymn books were quite good, so were some almanacs and catalogues but best of all was the tissue paper that oranges came wrapped up in. That was a real treat, but there wasn't a big enough supply.

Sometimes, paper for the privy was referred to as 'bum fodder' and we still use the word 'bumf' to describe a load of unwanted paperwork.

Tearing newspaper into squares was a job for the children in many families and they would learn from each other how many went into a bundle and how to make a hole with a meat skewer so a piece of string could be threaded through to hang it on a nail behind the privy door.

Proper toilet paper has been manufactured since the 19th century at first in packs called 'curl' papers because to a Victorian lady anything relating to the WC was unmentionable. Even then it was kept discreetly out of sight. It was well into the 20th century before we stopped using newspaper squares, except when we had guests – then we might splash out. Early toilet paper came in thin sheets, each one marked with a brand name, and was far too smooth and shiny. Guests probably yearned for a decent bit of newspaper, like they used at home. No wonder there were 'accidents' at some schools by children issued with just two or three sheets from a packet kept by the school teacher. Quick-witted boys were soon posing the question: 'What did the finger say to the lavatory paper?' Answer: 'You split and we're both in it.'

All sorts of things ended up in people's privies and a good example of this was a huge poster detailing the battle of Trafalgar that adorned the door of one used by Cyril Prouse's father-in-law, when he was a boy. He got to know so much about the famous battle he could reel off the names of the ships by heart.

This stood him in good stead at school where he got full marks for a composition.

Generally though, there is no doubt the bog standard privy was not 'user friendly' for children. The hole was cut to fit the largest backside not the smallest. Clinging to the edge of a privy seat, fearful of falling down that black hole, tended to keep small buttocks from relaxing and no doubt helped to sell laxatives. Privies large enough to have an adult and a child seat were ideal but not that common.

Comparatively speaking, toilet training today with a modern WC in a bathroom must be a piece of cake. Even so it can have complications if a story I picked up in Dunstable is anything to go by. It seems this man was very pleased with the way his wife had been teaching their little lad to go to the loo. He watched his son lift up the seat, then get a stool, and go like an adult. The only trouble was he used a piece of paper to finish off with so the chap told him that wasn't necessary and explained what men do. Next day when he got home from work his wife demanded an explanation because the boy had been doing what men do far too soon and so vigorously it was all over the bathroom floor.

[7]

PLAYGROUND PRIVIES

Privy standards in schools varied throughout the county and not many people looked back with fondness for them. At home use of the privy was restricted to members of the family, so it was a personal thing. At school communal use meant they were frequently misused, perhaps by small children unskilled in privy ways. Quite often they were placed across the playground as far away from the classroom as possible, which meant the children had to brave the elements, if they really could not wait until they got home. Doors tended to get left open and seats got wet, making the visit even more uncomfortable. Tiny windows at the back were commonly of the louvred style intended for ventilation rather than illumination so the average school privy was a dark and dingy place at best and absolutely foul at worst.

I came across inspectors' reports of 1904 that are critical of bucket privies being sited too *close* to school buildings and several are mentioned including one privy at a Henlow school which was only two yards from classroom windows. Another at Keysoe was just as bad in this respect, but, even worse, it was also too close to a well which supplied the drinking water.

Maulden school was held up as a good example of a managed system. Their privies were under cover but not near classrooms and access to them was through two cloakrooms where hats and coats could be hung and small hands washed. There were three privies for the girls, and one for the staff use on one side, and three on the other for boys, plus a urinal. They were all of a Moule Earth Closet design, with dry earth from a hopper covering the contents automatically with a sprung seat. The school was built by the Duke of Bedford in 1880 and he also provided

Before its closure the children attending Cardington village school would run across the yard to this privy block, boys on one side, girls on the other.

schools for seven other villages in Mid Bedfordshire. The Duke was a firm believer in the health and welfare of children and to combat the spread of disease like scarlet fever and diphtheria, which used to close the schools, he also donated the land on which Steppingley Isolation Hospital was built.

One man who started school at Maulden in 1937 remembers getting ill in a different way. 'We lived over a mile from the school and it took ages to walk home when we were small. Sometimes we took short cuts, which often turned out to be longer, and one of these was via George Street. In those days there was a tiny stream on the right which crossed a side road and was just about shoe deep. It was blistering hot on the day in question and that sparkling water was just too tempting to resist. It tasted good too – like forbidden fruit always does – but it was contaminated. The next day a huge swelling appeared "down below". Calling a doctor in pre National Health days was not done lightly so all the mothers in the row came to have a look and express their opinion. There was plenty of shaking of heads and tutting but nobody noticed the acute embarrassment being suffered, which lasted a lot longer than the complaint.'

The last word on Maulden school came by way of an admission that it was not rainwater that came over the urinal wall and landed in the girls' bicycle bay. Only a few boys could manage this feat but those that could had an enormous standing among their peers.

Mrs Dorothy Brooks explained what it was like at a school in Goldington when she was there. 'We had toilets that were like metal cans with wooden seats attached and once a week the "thunder" lorry would come to empty them and, if it was playtime, we were called back to our classrooms until it had gone.'

At Upper Sundon school there was a similar arrangement at the attached school-house where the headmistress lived. Bryan Smith was her nephew and, when he was a lad in the 1940s, used to cycle from Luton to visit her. 'Her loo was in a barn across the walled yard and consisted of a galvanised metal drum with a wooden seat and lid. The drum had a 4″ metal pipe coming out of the back which went up beyond a slated roof and terminated at a raised cowl. The walls were whitewashed brickwork and the wooden door was designed to let in plenty of fresh air – and cold. After use a little chemical was added from a small can, which helped to keep down the smell and emptying was done by the council workmen. At night a torch was essential because there was a pump standing over the well in the middle of the yard which you had to go round. Originally the well had an unusual mechanism; a continuous belt with small cups attached which, when a handle was turned, pulled water up from the depths and tipped it out through a spout. The school privies were at the far end of the walled playground, some for boys and some for girls, and were quite primitive, possibly draining to lower land which was always boggy.'

Generally speaking there was 'room for improvement' in our school privy days with perhaps a mark against those in charge saying 'could do better'.

[8]

THE STRAINS OF SERVICE LIFE

Some overseas arrangements can come as something of a shock even today but it was much worse for our troops serving abroad in World War II, as Cyril Prouse from Leighton Buzzard recalls from the time he was stationed in Algiers. 'We had taken over an old soldiers home and found that the two "footprints" over a hole affair was totally inadequate. It was necessary for the troops to dig a long trench in typical army fashion which would accommodate 30 men, in two rows of 15 – if they all needed to go at the same time. The biggest problem was the hordes of flies buzzing around, so we thought, but then a plague of locusts came down upon us, perhaps attracted to the camouflage netting, and after that the flies didn't seem so bad.'

Cyril also remembers travelling home from Italy after the war using trains with wooden seats and no toilets. Periodically the train would stop and passengers would pile out to buy food, find somewhere to have a wash and shave, and also join the queue for the toilet. The trouble was you never knew how long the train would stop for and, with just a quick toot on the whistle, it would pull away. It was obvious by the way people had to run along the platform yanking up their trousers, that the warning was totally inadequate – either that or the train driver had a strange sense of humour.

Brian Phillips' unit went to Cyprus and there the latrines were practically a route march from the camp. If you really needed to go at night you had to find your way in the dark to a row of purpose-built lavs, then turn round and back in because they were so small they were more like upturned boxes. You sat on a narrow wooden seat, hoping it was clean, then sang, or whistled

Remains of a latrine block at Twinwood Farm. Famous bandleader Glen Miller flew from here on his fateful journey to France in 1944.

a tune in case another soldier backed in thinking it was vacant and ended up on your lap.

Bob Peacock from Maulden remembers his army days too and the crude latrines they had to use. 'A trench was dug about four feet long by two feet wide, and two thick poles were fixed lengthways across the top from end to end. One pole was higher than the other so that a sort of cradle was formed to wedge your backside in. Unfortunately it was in the open, surrounded by a sacking screen, and when it rained these poles became really slippery. Unless you needed to go very badly it was not worth the risk in wet weather as falling in was a real possibility.'

Octogenarian Edgar Bratley from Meppershall recalls that latrines were a way of life for him in the army during World War II. He first saw action in France, at the time of Dunkirk, then became a desert-rat, was shipped to Italy and ended the war back in France. But there is one particular town in Italy that sticks in his mind because a large latrine was dug right in the town centre where roads converged. Here, behind hastily erected screens, great relief was found by the advancing allied army. Then, all at once, the order came to leave the town immediately, which is what they did. Edgar often wondered what the town thought of the 'present' they left and hoped they realised it was not the usual way the liberators left their mark.

The Royal Air Force also served overseas and Mr Alan Holloway, a former pilot officer, remembers his posting to Southern Africa. 'The ablution block was perfectly adequate but built so far away from the living quarters it just couldn't be used at night. To cater for the airmen's requirements after dark a large latrine bucket was placed midway between every two huts. In the morning they would be carted off and emptied.

'One evening a party of local girls were entertained in the mess and after dinner some walked around the camp with the young officers. A bright young girl asked about the huge buckets as they walked past and was told they were fire buckets. She took a quick peek inside the next one they came to and said "How can it be a fire bucket, it's empty?" Quick as a flash her young escort assured her it would be filled up during the night.'

It would seem the Royal Navy are lucky, they have water all around them so there should be no problem over loos, or 'heads' as the navy calls them. But ships go into dry dock and then, according to an ex-navy man from Bedford, life can become miserable. 'The only loos available were ashore in the dockyard so at night each mess deck throughout the ship received a cast iron latrine bucket.

'With twenty or more men to each bucket they usually got very full, sometimes brim-full. Each morning as soon as hammocks were stowed, two ratings in turn would man-handle the bucket up three or four flights of stairs, or ladders, struggle along numerous gangways, bumping over raised bases of watertight doors, get across the gangplank to the dockside and walk to the toilet block. The cast iron buckets were heavy, even when empty, they were back breaking when full. It was usual to slide a stick through the handle so that, with effort, it could be kept level when going up the stairs in the interest of the chap holding it up from below. It paid to be very careful because next week you were the man underneath – but accidents did happen. It was a recognised thing that anyone on latrine duty would not want their breakfast that day so it got shared amongst the rest.'

A final word on service lavs comes from photographer Tony Tacchi of Dunstable, who as a reserved 16 year old went to sea training school prior to joining the Merchant Navy. 'After being brought up to keep lavatorial matters strictly private, it was a terrific shock to find no doors on the toilets. Boys were sitting there, chatting, having a smoke and passing the time of day as if it was the normal thing to do. It was something I could never get used to.'

[9]

A CHANGE OF PACE

So here we are, at the beginning of a new millennium. We have long since relegated our old privies to the pages of history and, short of a major catastrophe, there is no reason why we should ever be reminded of the direct connection between sewage disposal and typhoid, typhus, smallpox, scarlet fever, diphtheria and cholera – which once plagued us.

It is hard to imagine a street in Luton just 146 years ago, which had 33 back-to-back houses sharing four privies. There was also an open cesspit close to a well. When cholera broke out, the fire brigade hosed the filth away and spread lime around the street to try to contain the disease. Bedford town centre also had cholera outbreaks in 1832 and 1849. The Mayor tried to help by issuing 'health hints'. Notices told people to clear filth away from their houses, keep their bedroom windows shut at night, wear flannel next to the skin and keep away from salads.

At this time neither town had a piped water supply and attempts to rectify this were actively opposed. At a council meeting in Bedford in 1859 the vote against waterworks was unanimous, even though many wells were contaminated and typhoid a regular visitor. Similarly in Luton where a decision was taken in 1861 that waterworks were not needed. It was supported by hundreds of ratepayers who had signed a petition to that effect.

In the mid 1860s, reformers finally won the day and by 1870 water had arrived on tap. With both towns becoming boards of health, sanitation was put under the spotlight. This instigated improvement schemes by the local authorities who remained responsible for these essential services right up to 1974 when reorganisation took place.

An old privy at Meppershall which served its purpose well.

A sewage treatment works catering for Flitwick and surrounding area.

Today, under Anglian Water, sewage treatment works cater for the county's sewage disposal needs. Slowly revolving sprinklers over filter beds are a common sight and a reminder that behind the scenes there is a silent service at work upon which we all depend. A cesspool emptying service also operates, particularly in isolated areas, but over 93% of households in the region are connected to main sewers which is amongst the highest levels in the world.

Spared until the end – privies on a demolition site in Luton captured on film by Jack Bean.

IT MAKES YOU THINK

In our fair county of Bedford, you can easily check it out,
There's over half a million souls and this without any doubt;
Now if we all do one and a quarter pounds of big jobs every day
That's 279 tons daily of solid waste – not sludge by the way.
If we multiply this sum by 365 to get one whole year's figure
Then we get a colossal 101.000 tons, actually even bigger.
How on earth can we visualise such a great pile? No panic,
Imagine something twice the size of the once mighty *Titanic*.

When mains water and sewerage arrived in some areas privies

close to houses could often be converted to WCs, which was convenient all round but, when they were put into houses, many people thought this was too filthy for words, after all you lived and ate your food in the house. Then barbecues became fashionable and it really seemed the world had gone topsy turvy – we were now eating outside and going to the loo inside. It took some getting used to and the term 'having the backdoor trots' for an upset stomach was no longer applicable.

People opposed to indoor loos would have been heartened by a report of experiments in 1966 which showed that flushing the loo created a 'bacterial aerosol' which, oddly enough, was even worse with both the seat and the lid down. Apparently the gap around the rubber buffers produced an effect which increased the pressure. Food for thought, no doubt.

FLITWICK MEMORIES

Well known Flitwick resident Mrs Bertha Mann, now over 90 years old, remembers going on the main sewers. She is glad she had the old privy turned into a WC. 'It saved climbing the stairs every time, especially when gardening and it was a boon when children visited. But the privy days are also keenly remembered. The lavender cart used to call about 9 o'clock and the man would bring his bucket to the privy, to save a double trip, then empty it into a tank pulled by a horse. This meant that the garden no longer benefited so if the horse did his business in the road this was collected up next morning and went round the roses. The milkman's horse did the same thing regularly further up the road, always in the same place and the man who lived there collected it religiously. One day, after the lavender cart had been the night before, there was a big pile right outside. As we were collecting it we saw the man running down the road

At over 90, Mrs Bertha Mann is glad she had her old privy in the garden converted into a proper loo.

with his bucket and spade so we got a move on and got the lot. Later we found the milkman had been a bit early that day and what we collected was from his horse. It was funny to see a man running after horse muck though!'

What wasn't funny was the time somebody left the lid off the well when children were in the yard. Mrs Mann and a friend nearly had a heart attack when they saw two toddlers sitting on the edge dangling their feet over the huge drop. Neither women dared make a sound in case it sent the children to their certain death; a silent move and a quick grab did the trick – then great relief as the lid was shut tight.

HAPPY DAYS IN MAULDEN

Bob Peacock of Maulden saw a few changes when he was a boy. 'We lived in a cottage that was the middle one of three with just one bucket privy between us. The other two cottages only had ladies living there so Dad was emptying the bucket very regularly. Then we moved to Maulden to get closer to the brickyards, where there was work, and that was the first time I saw a flush toilet. I had to be shown how to pull the chain but, once I got used to it, I loved to hear the water and looked forward to going.'

Sadly it did not last: a cheaper house became vacant down the road so they moved there pretty quick, back to the 'bucket and chuckit' method but at least it was their own privy. In due course they were served by the council's bucket-emptying service.

When Bob grew up and married he took a small cottage close by and that also had a privy down the garden. A public path passed within a few feet and his wife said she could see people clearly through the badly warped door. Bob assured her they couldn't see her and she believed him until a bucket-emptier said through the door, 'Don't hurry yourself Missus, I'm going

Model of an old privy from the Colourbox Collection.

to have my sandwiches and then I'll be back for your bucket.'

Bob was due to start his holidays the next day but had to spend the first part building a new privy, with close fitting door, exactly to his wife's requirements. After this they went away and had a great time. Many years later they were on holiday at the same place and Bob bought a model of an old privy, just like the one they had in their first cottage so many years before. His late wife gave it pride of place on the mantelpiece in their bungalow where it remains as a memory of those happy days.

Little John Northwood used to watch out for the tanker lorry from his front window in Maulden and study the men carrying the buckets to the hopper. His mother Margaret was always glad when they had gone as they would turn up when the bus was due. One day she was standing outside with relatives to see them off when the 'muck' wagon turned up. By the time the third bucket had been brought out from the houses, the smell drifting down on the group was so dreadful they were holding their noses. Then a bus full of people turned up to witness the event. Main sewers did not come a moment too soon in that road.

[1 0]

PRIVY PONDERINGS

Evacuees came as a bit of a shock to our rural system and the bucket emptying service felt the strain. Buckets needed emptying twice a week and a switch to day shift was noticed at Flitwick by Mrs Olive Richardson who wrote to say they always called at the worst possible time, like when the doctor was visiting.

'Previously the men had worked on a night cart. They were supposed to start at 10 o'clock but usually came earlier and when we were in our teens and reached courting stage we would be at the garden gate saying goodnight when in the middle of a romantic moment, a hoarse voice would shout "Mind your backs please." Those muck men and their smelly buckets must have ruined many a budding romance. In those days they carried lanterns and used a horse-drawn muck cart. They would fill up people's jam-jars with pink powder for sprinkling in the privy and, as soon as that was done, the horse would move on to the next gate without being told.'

As a small girl, Olive hated being enclosed in the privy and would leave the door open whatever the weather. The trouble was the privy faced the road so she was in full view of whoever looked over the low hedge. When she grew up and got married they moved into a larger house which had a privy with a trap-door at the back. This was easier on the bucket emptiers and less intrusive for the family though of course you had to make sure you knew when the men were coming to save any embarrassment. One day an aunt from Leicester came to stay and brought her own supply of toilet rolls with her, believing that bucket sanitation was bad enough let alone using newspaper squares. Unfortunately the family forgot to tell her about bucket empty-

Small, functional and sturdy – privies seen at Clapham.

ing day and she was on the seat when the trapdoor was whipped open and the bucket removed. Being on the heavy side she was not sprightly enough to leap off the seat so she stuck it out until she heard them replace the bucket. She was a jolly person and saw the funny side of it, deciding that the men must have thought the moon was out a bit early.

At Podington, Jack Bryan was telling me that he was 85 and reckoned he was the oldest man in the village. He remembers, as a small boy, playing at his grandfather's woodyard and being told the strange men there were German prisoners of war. He saw little of his own father who was a butcher on an ocean liner and often wondered what life would be like on one of those great ships.

Eventually Jack became a farm worker and lived in a cottage near the centre of the village. It had an outside privy and a bucket which you emptied yourself like most other people. There was a chap who would empty it for you for two shillings and sixpence and he got a lot of business in spite of the high price.

Mr and Mrs Taylor of Toddington used to live at Fancott, where they had a two-hole privy which, fortunately, is still there. It is a neat brick building with a slate roof, plastered ceilings and walls, and a brick-lined vault beneath the twin seats. On the frosted glass window is scratched 'C Carr 1899' and it is easy to imagine this Victorian farmer sitting there in quiet contemplation.

Mrs Taylor was raised on the farm and remembers the pit under the privy being emptied twice a year. 'The men would use a long-handled ladle and it would go into a tank on a cart pulled by a horse. It ended up on the fields where it was needed. Using the privy was a nuisance at night because you had to get practically dressed to cross the yard. There was nothing to fear even though a large boar was housed next to the privy.'

Amongst the shrubs: Mark Burley and Norma Congreve outside their 19th century privy at Fancott.

Two good seats over a substantial vault.

To many people, two-holers are a puzzle: were they for ladies too nervous to go on their own? Or were they for men who could have manly discussions without being overheard? Mr Taylor's answer – putting two seats in one privy saved the expense of another building – seems a very logical explanation.

Those were the days when water came from a well and the tin bath hung on a nail until needed. Mr Taylor noticed the contrast in the army during the war when he was stationed a few miles from a colliery in Nottinghamshire. The miners offered to share their facilities so the troops were briskly marched over and arrived soaked in sweat to enjoy the luxury of first class WCs and showers with lashings of hot water. Unfortunately they went back at the same fast pace so were sweatier than ever in the end. Perhaps the man in charge believed, like one of the Georgian royal dukes, that 'it was sweat that kept a man clean.'

Boys will be boys, they say, and it seems bucket emptiers were fair game in Mid Beds. At Westoning, P. Smith and his mates were no exception – they would watch the men bring their horse and tanker into the pub yard and put their lanterns around it before disappearing inside for a few pints. The boys would then unhook the buckets from under the tanker and turn them upside down over the lanterns, then wait for the confusion to start when the men came out of the pub in the dark.

At Steppingley, boys also harassed the bucket emptiers, Mr Jellis tells me. They would put a brick in the bucket to be emptied so that, not only did it cause a big splash when one bucket was poured into the other but the brick had to be removed before its contents could be tipped into the tanker. Even worse was a craze Millbrook boys had for opening the trapdoor at the back of the privy when somebody was on the seat, and shoving in a stinging nettle. It was certainly no joke, according to Mrs Phillimore of Ampthill.

On the subject of boys' exploits, the five Flitwick teenagers who went down the sewers in the village in May 1979 caused quite a commotion. Neither the police nor members of the public could get them out so firemen using breathing apparatus were called in. The boys had travelled quite a distance heedless of sudden flooding or dangerous fumes that could have caused a tragedy.

Anne Slack of Flitwick learned that children at Toddington had a special song they used to sing when the bucket emptiers came around:

> 'The night cart was full, right to the brim
> The driver fell in and couldn't swim
> He sank right to the bottom
> Just like a blooming stone
> And now you can hear him singing
> There's no place like home.'

Mrs Lilian Marchant of Sharnbrook is 90 years old and moved into her present home from Somerset in 1931. The little detached building at one side contained the privy, a copper for heating water and a tin bath. A well, behind the cottage, supplied their water.

Lilian's late husband Ron used to empty the privy bucket in the garden, organising it properly so each part received its share and it thrived. 'When the council's emptying scheme started most people were enthusiastic, but after the men had spilt some of the bucket's contents a couple of times, getting it out of its corner position, Ron went back to doing it himself and the garden was not deprived after all.

'A friend who came to visit Ron once was so aghast at finding such a basic privy he said he could never visit again. The thought of using a bucket that Ron had to empty was more than he could

An unusual arrangement of a wash-house cum privy at Sharnbrook. Mrs Lilian Marchant moved into the cottage in 1931 and raised her family here.

stand.' Lilian believes the rural way of life did the family no harm: they all lived happy and healthy lives.

It was very different for people at Coffle End, Sharnbrook, in 1871. According to records, there were 68 people living in a cluster of tiny cottages, sharing just two bucket privies. These were emptied in a nearby open sump and the contents slowly drained down a ditch into the river. Disease was a constant visitor and one poor couple, the Partridges, buried all six of their children through typhoid. Lilian remembers years ago that people called the place 'Coffin End', no doubt in view of its history, but today Coffle End is an impressive example of how ancient cottages can be transformed into highly desirable residences.

Weighing 28lbs when full, these old china slop pails were not particularly user friendly.

Mrs Mary Abbott was an only child at Houghton Conquest but later became the eldest of five children and able to help around the house. 'Emptying chamber pots was the worst job because the slop-pail had to be tipped into a pit right down the garden. It was often slippery on the unmade path and accidents happened even with the anti-splash device in place. Sometimes accidents happened inside the house as well, especially when a younger sister was helping. Fortunately lino was waterproof which allowed a bit of leeway in dashing for the mop.'

Mary was again reminded of the old privy days when, years later, her husband Dennis started bringing home council sewage tankers and leaving them outside the house, just as if they were still on the bucket. It was convenient for him because he was servicing them and a run home at lunchtime gave them a road test – however unpopular.

P.J. Davis writes from Hockliffe about a 'dry earth closet' he once used during the war. The hopper at the back was full of wood ash and was operated by pulling a brass handle set into the toilet seat. He was told that the wood-ash acted as a disinfectant and reduced the smell. Later, at his father's pub, he had the unenviable job of emptying the buckets from a 'three-holer' reserved for lady customers. It was hard for him to decide which was worse – digging the hole or carrying the buckets.

A story that has circulated for years concerned a lady visiting this country who rented a small cottage but could not find the privy, so she wrote to the owners discreetly asking where the 'place of easement' was. They were not familiar with the term 'place of easement' and did not connect it to the ivy-covered privy right down the bottom of the garden. As the term she used sounded restful they assumed she meant a church or

A relic from the past – an old pub privy found at Milton Ernest.

chapel. Knowing where there was one, they wrote back telling her the nearest 'place of easement' to the cottage was five miles away in such a beautiful spot people usually took their sandwiches and made a day of it. The seats were plush and the children sang during the proceedings. 'Sadly it is not open every day', the letter continued, 'which may be a problem if you are used to going regularly. Also it does get crowded, even though it seats fifty, so you may have to stand. This happened to my poor wife, after rushing to get there, which is the reason we haven't been for six months and it pains us very much.

'We hope this will assist you; please note, hymn sheets are hanging behind the door.'

[11]

A Privy Poem

Most of our privies have now gone west
But some of us think those days were best;
Private time and a good place to think
And who would care if you made a stink?

A spider, or two, lurked under the seat
But only to catch flies they needed to eat;
Much worse than creepy crawlies by far
Was someone who left the privy door ajar.

When winter snow covered the garden at night
The privy looked lovely under its cap of white;
No frosted glass there to hide nature's display
Like the modern bathrooms in our homes today.

A man needed a garden, with a family to keep
But without manure could neither sow nor reap;
Just emptying the bucket was all that was needed
And the bonus was crops that were never seeded.

So our old garden privies made very good sense
Most were strongly built, at no great expense;
They served us well the way they were meant,
So, for thee, my poor privy, I must lament.

This tiny privy, found at Caldecote, has a roof which slopes the same way as the barn it is attached to.

A PRIVY BY ANY OTHER NAME

A puzzle to end with. Why all those euphemisms for the humble lavatory? Here we are in the 21st century still 'washing our hands', or 'spending a penny'. Oddly enough, some of our alternatives are much more likely to raise an eyebrow than the word we are trying to avoid. However, without trying to reason why, here is a collection of lavatory nicknames, by no means complete.

A certain place
Asterroom
Aunties
Backroom
Bog
Boghouse
Bombay
Chamber of Commerce
Chamberlain pianos (bucket lav)
Closet
Comfort station
Crapphouse
Crapping Castle
Crapping kennel
Dike
Dinkum dunnies
Dunnekin
Dunnick
Dyke
Doneks
Dubbs

Duffs
Garden loo
Garderobe
Gong
Gong house
Heads
Here it is
Holy of Holies
Home of rest
Honk
House of Commons
House of relief
Houses of Parliament
Jakes
Jericho
Jerry-cum-tumble
John
Karzi
Klondyke
Larties
Latrine
Lats

Lav
Library
Little boys' room
Little girls' room
Little room
Long drop
Loo
My aunts
My uncles
Nessy
Netty
Out the back
Petty
Place of easement
Place of repose
Place of retirement
Powder room
Reading room
Reredorter
Round the back
Shittus
Shooting gallery
Shot tower
Shunkie
Slash house
Smallest room
The back house
The boggy
The dunny
The end

The offices
The thingumejig
The throne room
The whatjacallit
The wee house
Thunderbox
Urinal
Watering hole
Waterloo
Windsor Castle
'Yer tiz'

Favourite excuses

I must:
    go for a Jimmy Riddle
    go for a Tom Tit
    go to pick daisies
    go to the Grove
    go where the wind always
        blows
    pluck a rose
    powder my nose
    see a man about a dog
    shake hands with an old
        friend
    spend a penny
    stack my tools
    wash my hands
    water my horse
    water my garden
    water my leeks